STRINGSTASTIC
Level 3
VIOLA

By Lorraine Chai
USA Edition

PO BOX 815 Epping NSW 1710 Australia
www.stringstastic.com
Copyright © 2019 Lorraine Chai
First Published 2019
2nd Edition 2020
USA Edition 2021

Book design by Meilisa Lengkong

All rights reserved.
Reproduction in whole or in part for any use whatsoever is strictly prohibited.

THE AUTHOR
LORRAINE CHAI

Lorraine is a multi talented instrumentalist and an international educator. She graduated from the Sydney Conservatorium of Music with a Bachelor of Music Studies in 2008 and completed her Graduate Diploma of Education at the Australian Catholic University a year later.

Having grown up with a musical family, Lorraine began piano lessons at the age of four and violin at the age of six, giving her first violin performance at just seven years of age. Lorraine started teaching violin at the age of 14 and founded a string ensemble at her local church. From there, teaching and performing became her passion.

Lorraine loves finding new and exciting ways students can learn their instrument in a classroom setting as well as in private lessons. Along her musical journey and exposure to the various educational methods including Kodaly, Suzuki, Orff, and Dalcroze, Lorraine has also attended Alexander Technique workshops, and has found that she can integrate these various methods into her own teaching technique for the benefit of her students.

Lorraine has extensive ensemble and orchestral experience in Malaysia and in Australia. Lorraine currently the Music Director of Stringstastic Pty Ltd and is an active member with the Australian Strings Association, AUSTA NSW. She also co-ordinates instrumental programmes and runs string ensembles for some of Sydney's most celebrated schools.

PREFACE

Stringstastic viola Level 3 follows on from the knowledge which young players have gained in Stringstastic viola Level 1 and Level 2. Stringstastic viola Level 3 extends that knowledge through games and fun graphics to assist young beginner violists to help them better understand the instrument and to learn music theory in an enjoyable way.

This Stringstastic series can be used in a private lesson or along side the violin and cello book series in a classroom setting.

For extra resources, go to www.stringstastic.com to download them for free.

Have fun!!

ACKNOWLEDGEMENT

This book was made possible with the encouragement of my family and loved ones. I would like to thank the following for their advice and input in making this book possible.

Dr. Rita Crews OAM, FMusA (honoris causa), PhD(UNE), BA(Hons), AMusTCL, GradCertDistEd (UNE), FMusicolASMC, HonFNMSM, DipMus (honoris causa) (AICM) MIMT, MACE, MMTA, JP.

Mary Nemet AMusA, is a prominent string educator, AMEB Examiner, Reviews Editor for AUSTA Stringendo and contributor to Strings USA.

Helen Tuckey PG Dip Music (Manhattan School of Music), AMusA, MIMT, DipArts(music) (Victorian College of the Arts)

CONTENTS

- 4 — REVISION
- 7 — NOTE AND REST VALUES
- 11 — NEW TIME SIGNATURE
- 15 — READING RHYTHMS
- 18 — RELATIVE MINORS AND MAJORS
- 21 — MINOR SCALES
- 26 — MINOR ARPEGGIOS
- 28 — LABELING SCALES AND ARPEGGIOS
- 29 — WHAT HAVE WE LEARNED SO FAR?
- 31 — OSTINATO
- 32 — SEQUENCE
- 33 — ITALIAN TERMS
- 35 — COMPOSITION
- 37 — ANACRUSIS
- 39 — 3RD POSITION
- 42 — LAST REVISION
- 44 — TEST

STRINGSTASTIC

Revision

Let us revise naming the notes on the alto clef. A reminder that we only use the first 7 letters of the alphabet. After G the note goes back to A.

Notes on the open strings

Cute   Girl   Dances   Around

Notes in between

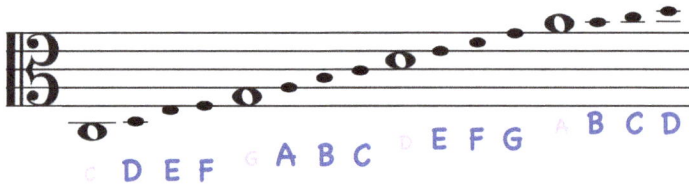

Notes through the lines

Fat   Alley   Cats   Eat   Garbage

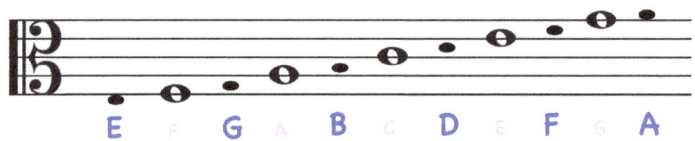

Name these notes without looking back to the top of the page.
(Use capital letters.)

D

In first position, write out the fingering above the notes in the question above.

Name the string where each of these notes can be found.
(Careful with the fingering. Some are lowered.)

① ② ③	F	C String
① ② ③	B♭	
① ② ③	G	
① ② ③	E♭	
① ② ③	B	

① ② ③	A	
① ② ③	D	
① ② ③	C	
① ② ③	C	
① ② ③	F	

In whole notes, draw THREE different C sharps.

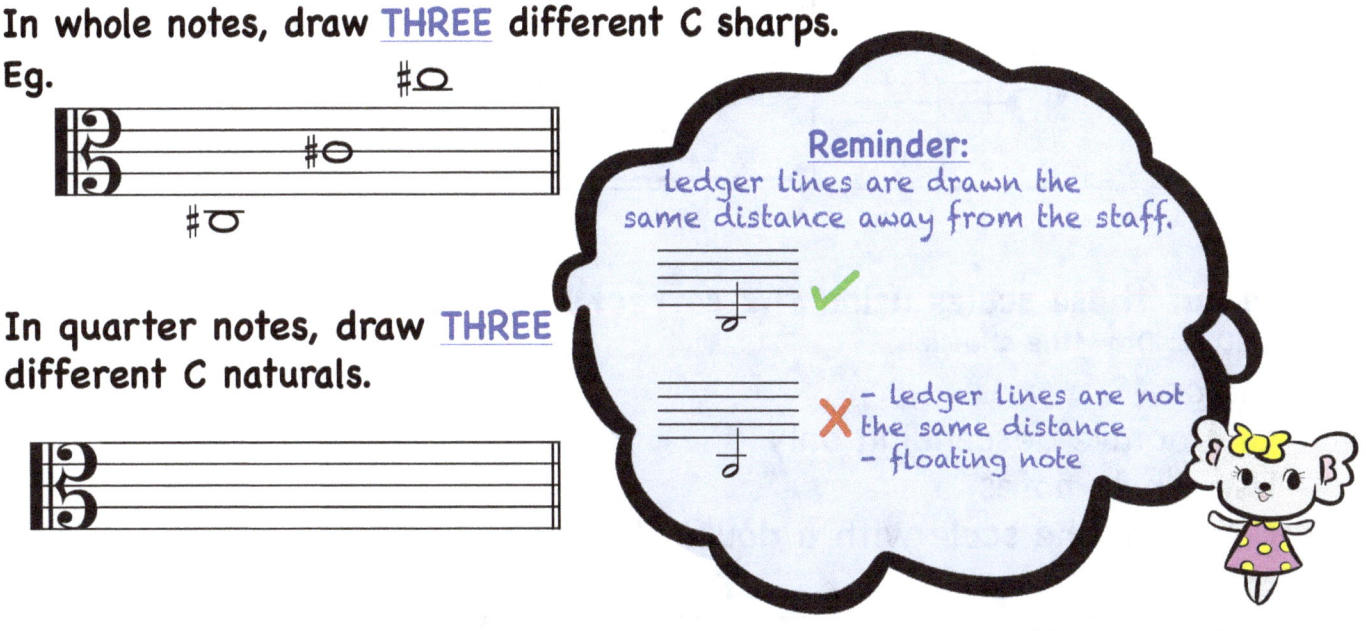

Reminder: ledger lines are drawn the same distance away from the staff.

✓

✗ - ledger lines are not the same distance
- floating note

In quarter notes, draw THREE different C naturals.

Reminder: ALWAYS draw the ledger lines first, before the note.

In whole notes, draw THREE different E flats.

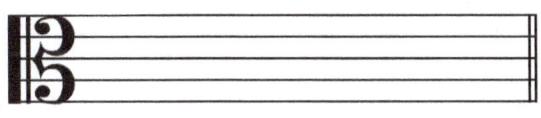

In half notes, draw THREE different D flats.

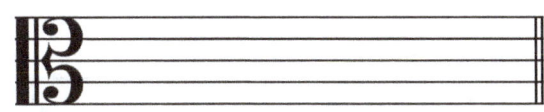

Answer the questions in each square.

a. Draw a note that can be played on the open string and using the 4th finger.
b. Draw the key signature of D major.
c. Place a fermata sign on the note.
d. Show that the next note is a half step higher.
e. Name the symbol.
f. Name the key signature.
g. Place a tie in a suitable place.
h. Draw 2 eighth notes beamed together.
i. Name this note.
j. Place an accent on this note.
k. Circle the correct italian word that means at a walking pace.
l. Draw a whole note rest.
m. Show the time signature representing 3 quarter beats in a measure.
n. Draw a slur over the notes.
o. What is the value of this rest?

Write out these scales using the correct key signature.
(REMINDER: Draw the alto clef.)

D major
- One octave descending only
- Use whole notes
- Complete the scale with a double bar line

C major
- One octave in an ascending and descending order
- Use half notes
- Complete the scale with a double bar line

Note and Rest Values

NAME	NOTE	REST	NOTE VALUE
Sixteenth note	♪ ← double tail	double tail → 𝄿	$1/4$
2 sixteenth notes joined	← beam		$1/4 + 1/4 = 1/2$
4 sixteenth notes joined			1
Dotted quarter note	♩.		$1\ 1/2$

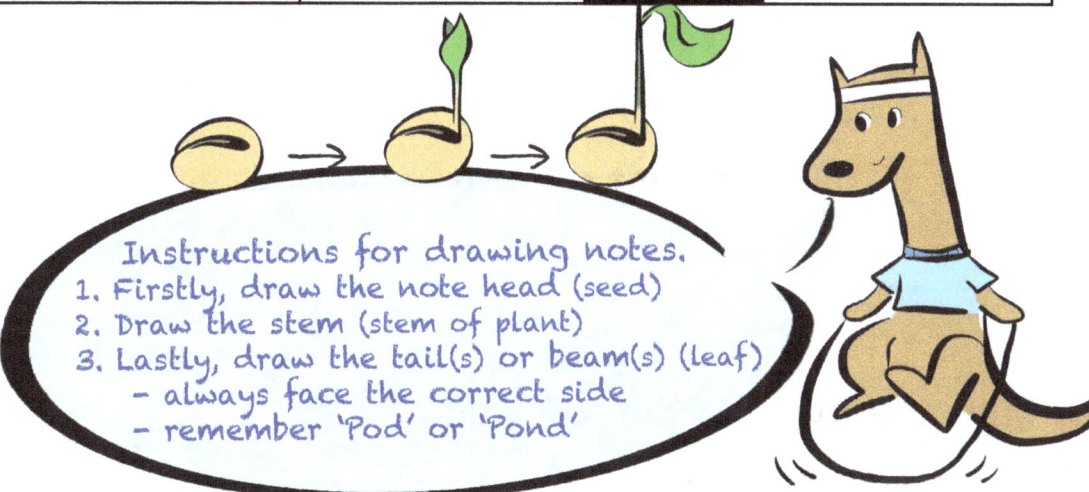

Instructions for drawing notes.
1. Firstly, draw the note head (seed)
2. Draw the stem (stem of plant)
3. Lastly, draw the tail(s) or beam(s) (leaf)
   - always face the correct side
   - remember 'Pod' or 'Pond'

Draw the tail for each of these notes and rests and write its value.

Sixteenth Note

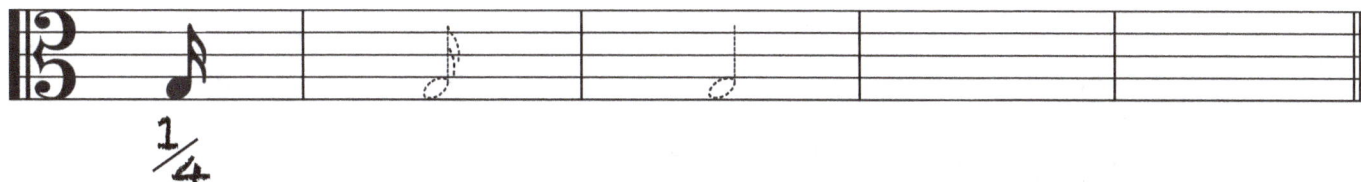

$1/4$

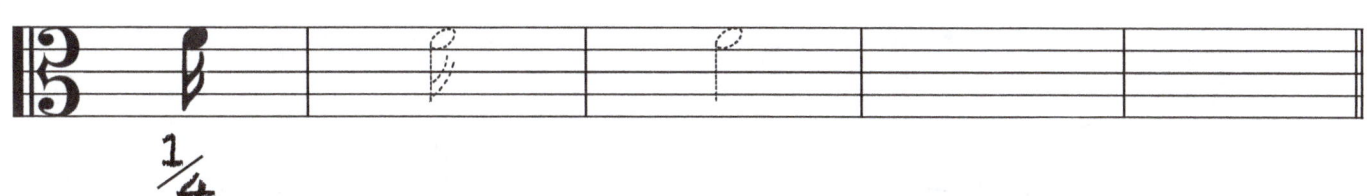

$1/4$

Sixteenth Note Rest *(draw a dot in the middle 2 spaces)*

$1/4$

8

Draw TWO sixteenth notes beamed together.

How many quarter note beats are 2 sixteenth notes worth?

Draw FOUR sixteenth notes beamed together.

How many quarter note beats are 4 sixteenth notes worth?

A. **Figuring out the dotted value.**

𝅗𝅥. = The note itself + ¹/₂ value of itself

𝅗𝅥 + ¹/₂ 𝅗𝅥

2 + 1 = __3__

𝅘𝅥. = 𝅘𝅥 + ¹/₂ 𝅘𝅥

1 + ¹/₂ = __1¹/₂__

(The dot next to the note means ¹/₂ the value of itself.)

B. **Eighth note value.**

1 eighth = ¹/₂ count

2 eighth notes = 1 count

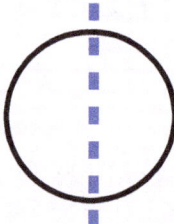

Think of a quarter note as being like a cake or a circle. When we cut it in halves, we have 2 eighths (2 halves of a full cake). When we put them back together, it becomes 1 full circle again.

C. **Sixteenth note value.**

A sixteenth note has 2 tails and is a smaller note value then an eighth note, hence they are quicker notes.

1 sixteenth note = $\frac{1}{4}$ count

2 sixteenth notes = $\frac{1}{2}$ count

4 sixteenth notes = 1 count

As you can see on the diagram on page 10, we need 4 sixteenth notes to create a quarter note which is a total value of 1 count.

Add the total number of quarter beats in these note values.

Eg. 3 + ½ = 3 ½ quarter beats

How many quarter note beats do these notes need to create the same value?

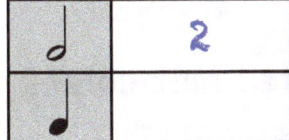

How many eighth note beats do these notes need to create the same value?

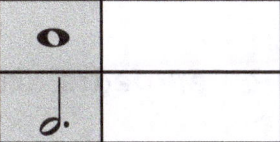

Below is a diagram which shows the number of notes of different lengths which is equal in value to a whole note.

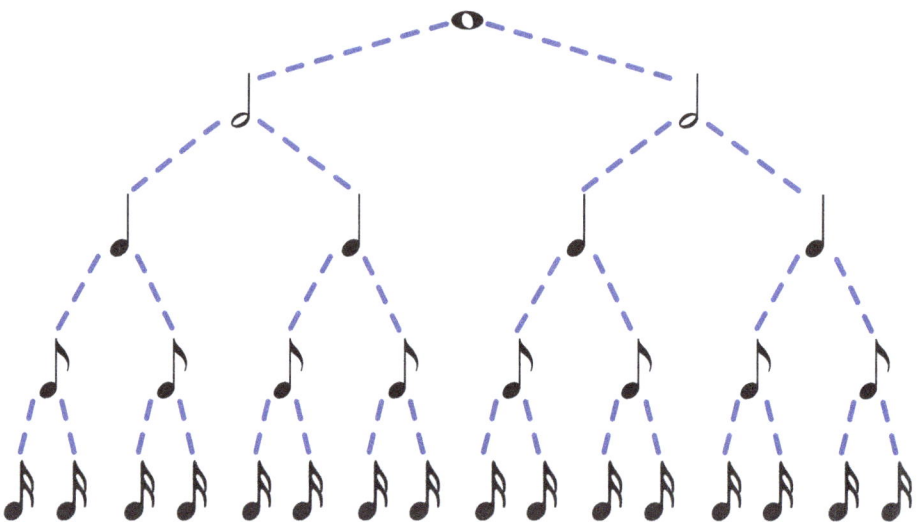

Answer the questions below.

a. How many quarter beats are there in a whole note? 4

b. How many eighth beats are there in a half note?

c. How many eighth beats are there in a whole note?

d. How many quarter beats are there in a dotted half note?

e. How many sixteenth beats are there in an eighth note?

f. How many eighth beats are there in a dotted quarter note?

g. How many sixteenth beats are there in a dotted quarter note?

h. How many sixteenth beats are there in a half note?

i. How many dotted quarter beats are there in a dotted half note?

j. How many sixteenth beats are there in a whole note?

k. How many half beats are there in a whole note?

l. How many sixteenth beats are there in a half note tied with an eighth note?

New Time Signature

The time signature which we have learned so far has the number 4 at the bottom which shows that we should count in quarter beats.

4 → number of beats per measure
(4) → 4 = quarter beats per measure

In the diagram on page 10, we see that we need 4 quarter beats to make a whole note, hence the bottom of the time signature is 4 which shows us that we should count each measure in quarter beats.

In this book, we will learn to change the number on the bottom of the time signature.

1. $\frac{6}{\circled{8}}$ → looking back at the diagram, we need 8 eighth notes to make a whole note. Hence, <u>8 means eighth beats.</u>

$\frac{6}{8}$ means there are 6 eighth beats in each measure. The eighth notes here are grouped in THREEs and beamed together.

When using rests in $\frac{6}{8}$, use TWO eighth rests where there are TWO eighth beats of silence. This helps us remember to count in eighth beats.

THREE eighths are worth a dotted quarter beat. Hence if you have THREE eighth rests, you can use 𝄽·.

2. $\frac{2}{②}$ → looking back at the diagram, we need 2 half notes to make a whole note. Hence, 2 means half note beats.

The note and rest grouping in this time signature is the same as the note grouping we have learnt even though this is in half beats.

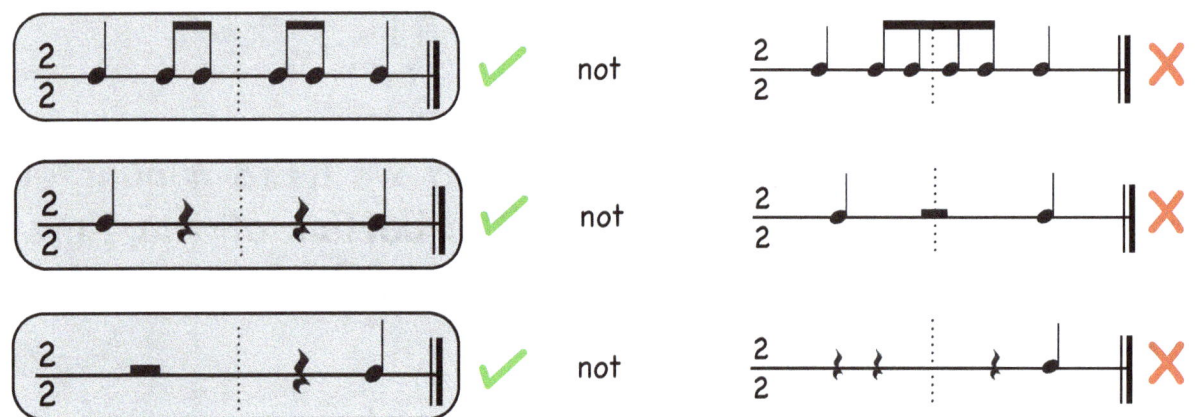

Complete the following measures with rests.

Sometimes we can write our time signatures differently.

$\frac{4}{4}$ = C

$\frac{2}{2}$ = ¢

Summary of different time signatures.

$\frac{2}{2}$	$\frac{2}{4}$	$\frac{6}{8}$
2 **half** beats in a bar	2 **quarter** beats in a bar	6 eighth beats in a bar grouped in **dotted quarter** beats
♩ ♩	♩ ♩	♩. ♩.
eighth notes grouped in **FOURS**	eigth notets grouped in **PAIRS**	eighth notes grouped in **THREES**
♫♫ ♫♫	♫ ♫	♫♫ ♫♫

Write out the correct beats of each measure and join the notes with a beam to show the correct number of beats per measure.

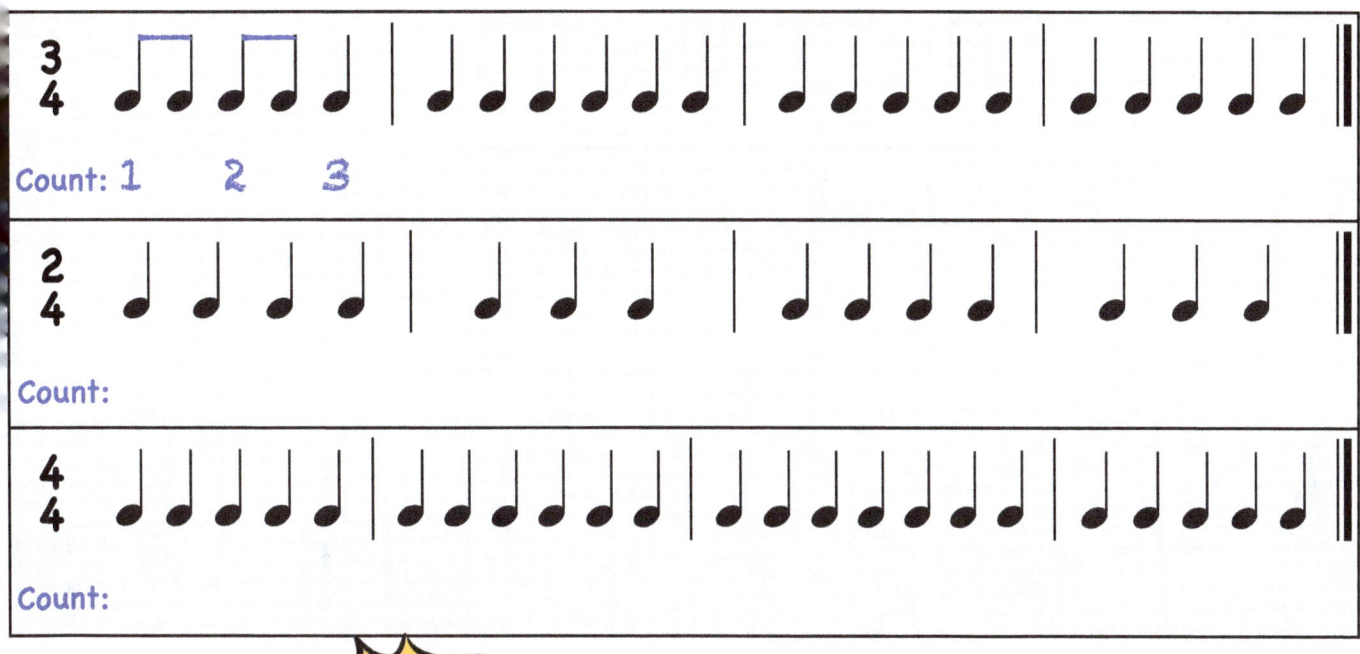

Write out the correct beats of each measure and change the values with either one of the actions below to show the correct number of beats per measure. Add...
1. a dot after the note
2. a tail or two
3. a beam
4. color note head

14

Tommy has decided to give up his bug collection and is releasing them in his back garden. See if you can spot the different colored bugs as they go free.

TIME SIGNATURE	COLOR
3/4	RED
6/8	BLUE
2/2 or ¢	GREEN
2/4	YELLOW

How many bugs are there in the following?

Red -

Blue -

Green -

Yellow -

Reading Rhythms

Rhythm is the most important thing in music as it defines the way a piece is to be played.

Beat vs. Rhythm

Beat is a constant pulse like a heart beat or a ticking clock.

Rhythm is a pattern of different note values where the length of each note can vary.

Rhythms can be read in a number of ways. See below for various approaches that can be used.

Notes	French Time Names	Hungarian Time Names	Standard Counting
♩	ta	ta	1
♫	ta te	ti ti	1 n
♬♬	ta-fa te-fe	ti-ka ti-ka	1-e n-a
♩♫	ta te-fe	ti ti-ka	1 n-a
♫♩	ta-fa te	ti-ka ti	1-e n

Below are a few rhythmic notations to practice by clapping and saying aloud the prefered rhythmic names. *Eg. ta- te, tafa tefe, etc* if using the french names.

(**NOTE:** The rhythmic notation below has no note heads, hence are known as stick notations.)

A. | | | |
　 ⊓ | | ⊓
　 | | | ⊓
　 ⊓ ⊓ ⊓ |

B. | ⊓ | |
　 ⊓ | | ⊓
　 | ⊓ | ⊓
　 ⊓ ⊓ | |

C. | ⊓ | |
　 ⊞ | | ⊓
　 | ⊞ | ⊞
　 ⊓ | ⊓ |

16

D. | ♩♩ | | E. | ♫♩ | | F. | ♫♫ |
♬ | | ♫   ♬ | ♫ | ♬ | | ♬
| ♬♬ | | ♫♬ | | ♫ | ♫
♬♬ | ♫ | ♬♬ | ♫ | ♬♬♬ |

> **More printable rhythmic dictations and flashcards are available at www.stringstastic.com**

We can also read rhythms by using words.
Each note can be repesented by a word based on the number of notes. The more notes the more syllables.

Write out as many word(s) as you know to match the rhythm given in each box below.

♩ cat slow crawl Bob	♫ co-py	♬
♩ ♩ but-ter scotch	♬♬ ca-ter-pil-lar	♩ ♫
♩ ♫ goose-ber-ry	♩ ♫ ♫	♬♬ ♫

Using the words you collected from the page before, create your own rhyme with the rhythms given below.

crawl Bob crawl

In quarter note beat value, fill in the missing time signatures in the question above.

Now try and play the rhythm above with your viola using the words you have written down.
(Saying the words out loud while playing can help you play correctly.)

Relative Minors and Majors

Just as you have direct relatives in your family, major keys have minor keys who are relatives - think of it as your relatives that share the same surname as you do.
The major and relative minors share the same key signature.

From Level 2, we learn that C major has no sharps or flats in its key signature. C major's relative minor key is A minor. Therefore A minor also does not have any sharps or flats in its key signature.

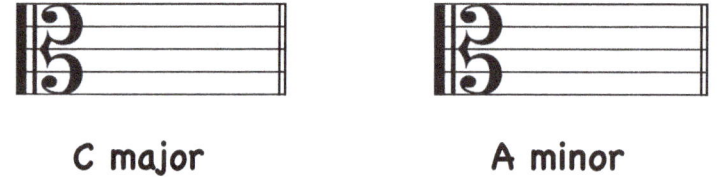

C major   A minor

Try memorizing that C major is related to A minor.

There are a few ways of finding out the relative minors of the major keys. Let us look at your fingerboard and find the note A and C.

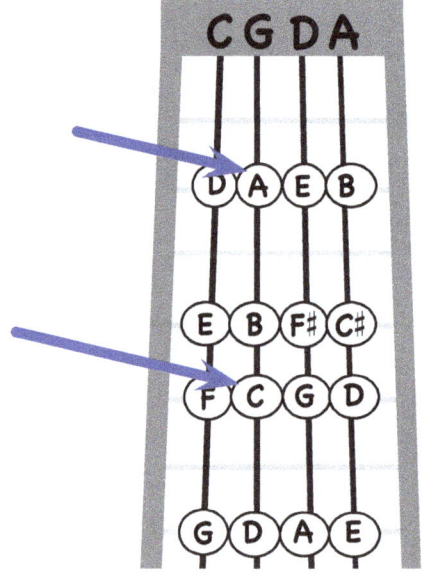

Let us look at how many steps it takes from the note C to A.

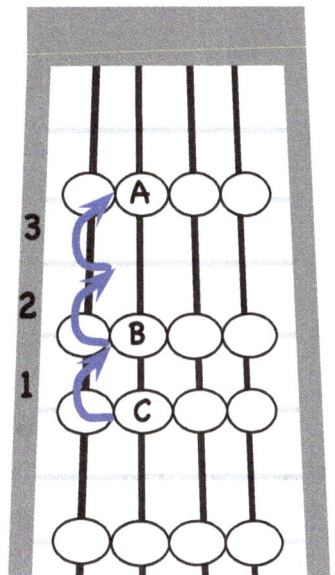

It only takes 3 half steps backwards from C to A.

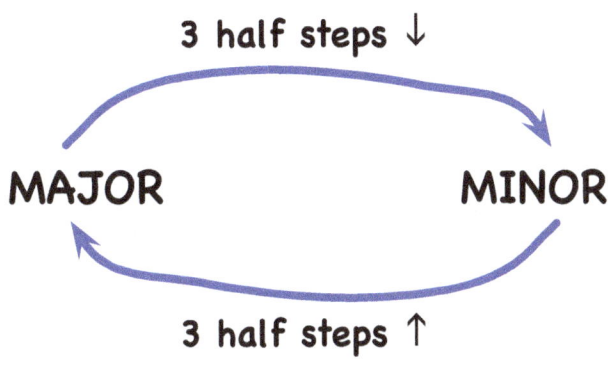

Hence the relative minors for the major scales we have learned are as below.

C major ⟶ A minor

G major ⟶ E minor

D major ⟶ B minor

Check on the fingerboard in the previous page to see if the related minors for the major scales above are correct.

Below is how the key signature would look for each related key.

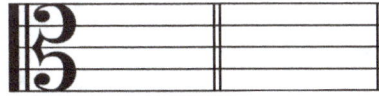
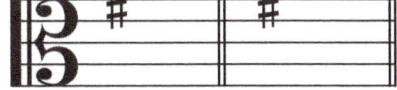
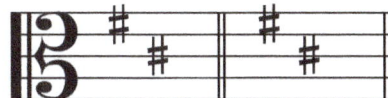

20

Draw the key signature for these keys.

D major   A minor   G major   B minor   E minor

The scales and arpeggios below are missing their key signature. Using the key signatures we have learned up till now, draw the appropriate key signature and figure out if they are in a major or minor scale.

Eg.

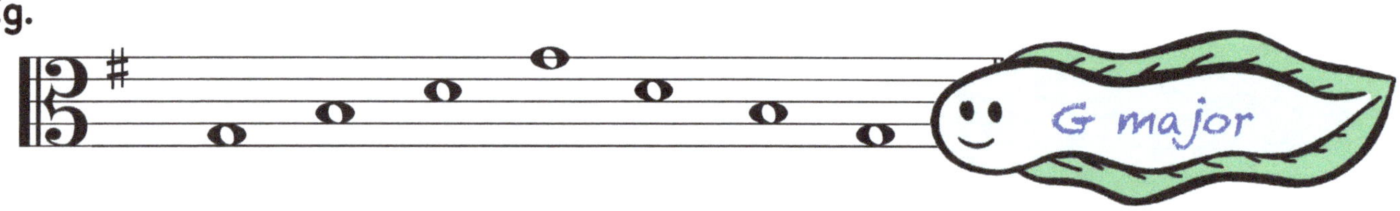

G major

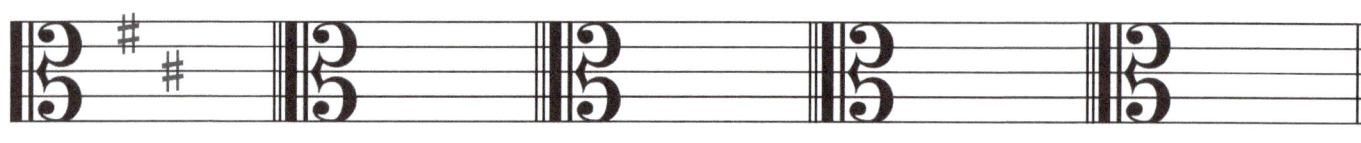

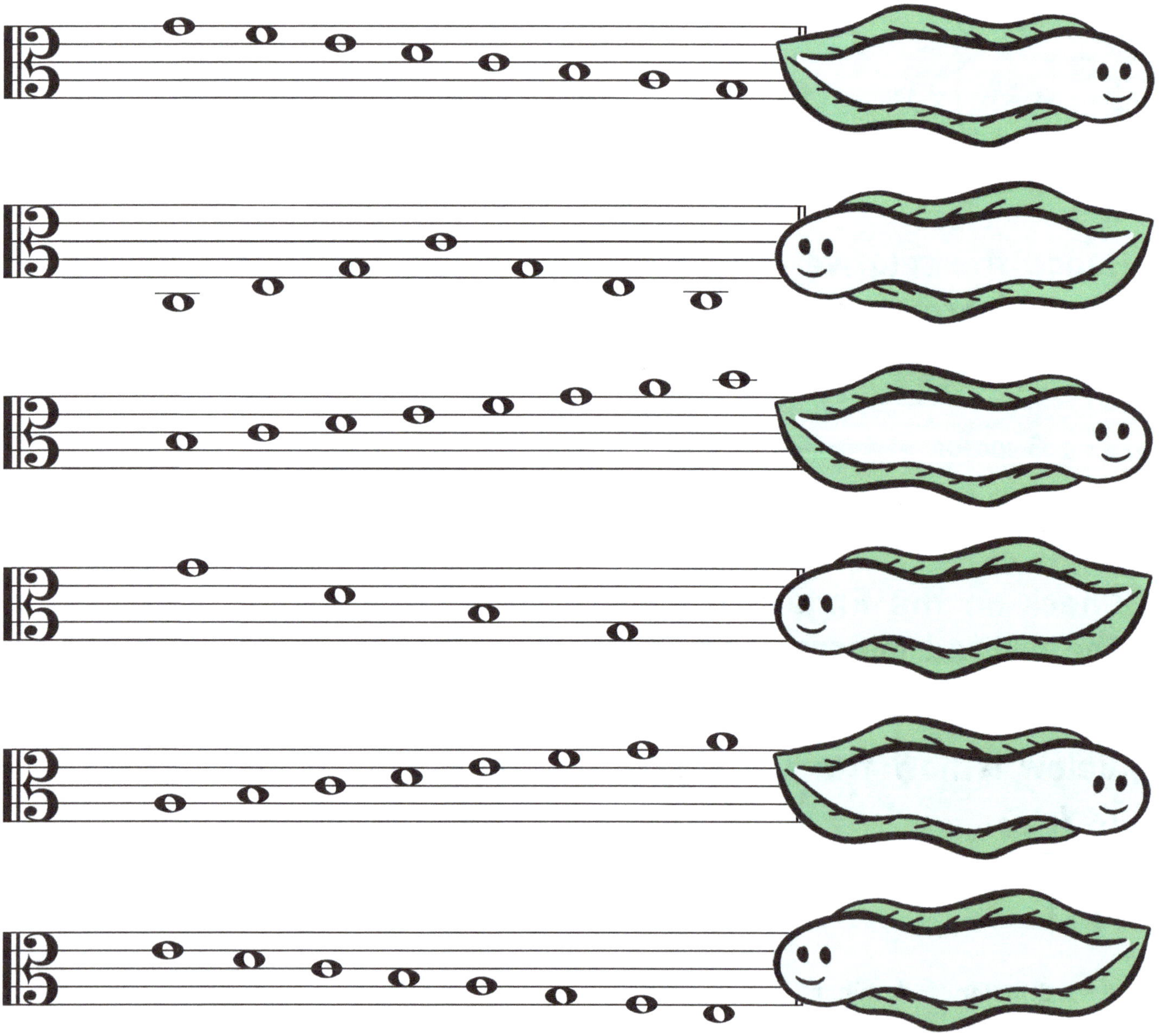

Minor Scales

The difference between a major and minor scale is that major sounds happy and minor sounds sad.

Major 😊
Minor ☹️

There are 3 different quality types of minor scales.

MINOR — natural
        harmonic
        melodic

It is very easy to remember the difference between the three minor scales.

natural - normal (NO change)

Now look at the first letter of the next 2 minor scales (harmonic and melodic). How many curves does the letter have?

harmonic - 1 hump/curve = 1 change
raise the 7th note

Melodic - 2 humps/curves = 2 changes
raise the 6th & 7th note going up ↑
lower the 6th & 7th note going down ↓

A natural minor

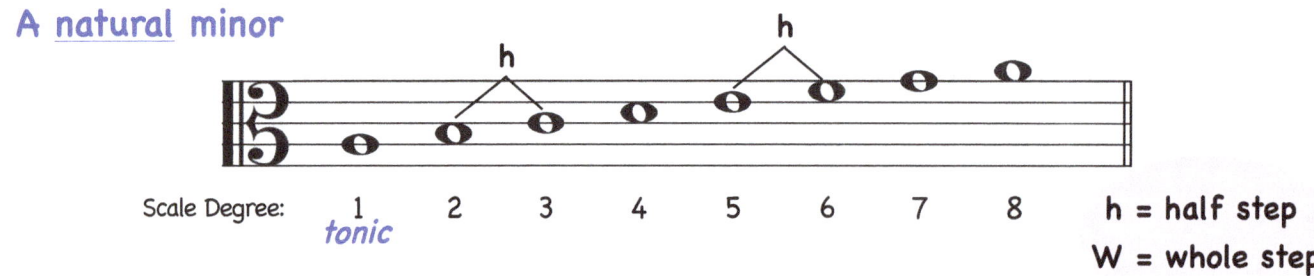

Scale Degree: 1 (tonic), 2, 3, 4, 5, 6, 7, 8

h = half step
W = whole step

The whole-half step pattern of any natural minor scale is as below,

W - h - W - W - h - W - W

Between which scale degree numbers are the half steps?

____-____ and ____-____

A harmonic minor

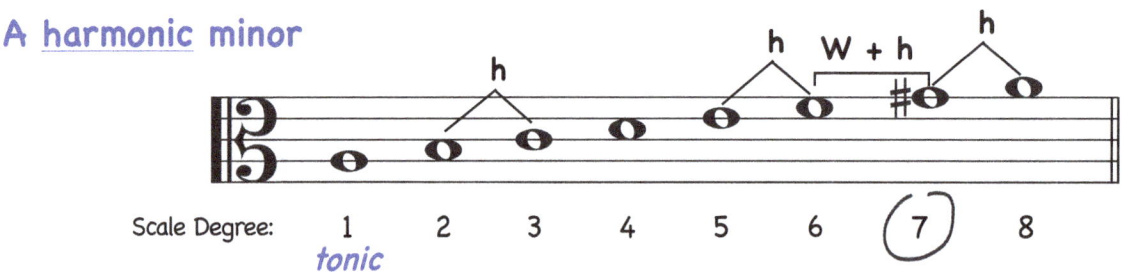

Scale Degree: 1 (tonic), 2, 3, 4, 5, 6, ⑦, 8

raise the 7th note ↑
(there is always a (whole + half step) pattern in a harmonic scale)
6th & 7th degrees

The whole-half step pattern of any harmonic minor scale is as below,

W - h - W - W - h - (W+h) - h

Between which scale degree numbers are the half steps?

____-____ , ____-____ and ____-____

How many types of minor scales are there?

Name all the different quality types of minor scales available.

_____

_____

_____

Change these natural minors into harmonic minors.
(**HINT:** Raise the 7th degree.)

A harmonic minor

(**REMINDER:** Count the scale degree from the lowest note.)

Name the scales above.

Now try playing these harmonic scales on your viola.

24

Lastly let us see what a melodic minor scale looks like.

A melodic minor

Scale Degree: 1 2 3 4 5 (6 7) 8 (7 6) 5 4 3 2 1
tonic

raise the 6th & 7th note going **up** ↑
lower the 6th & 7th note going **down** ↓

In half notes, write a ONE octave minor scale in an ascending and descending order.
(**REMINDER:** Sometimes you need to add accidentals.)

B harmonic minor
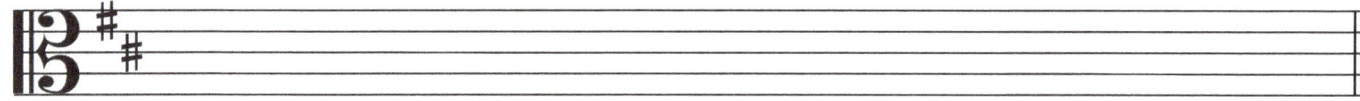

A natural minor
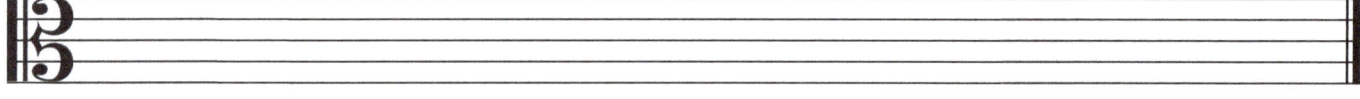

E natural minor
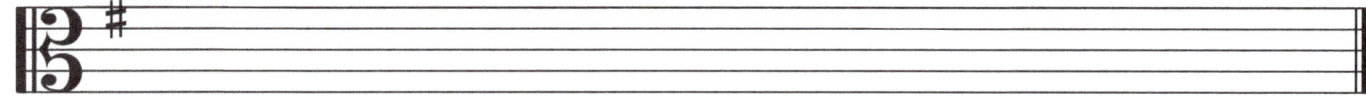

E harmonic minor
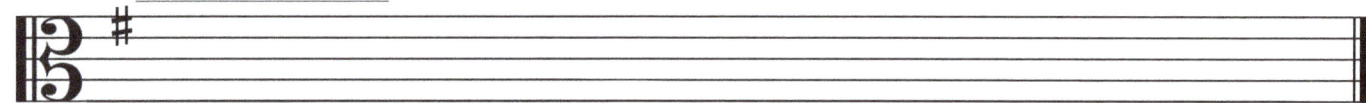

B melodic minor
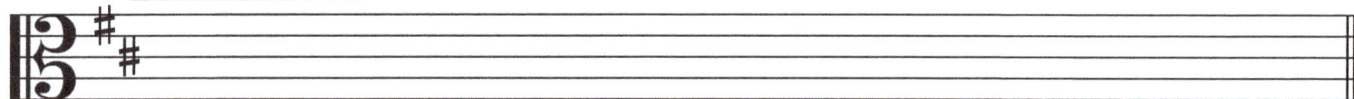

**Now try playing these scales on your viola.
Can you hear the difference between the natural, harmonic and melodic minor scales?**

B natural minor

A harmonic minor

E melodic minor

A melodic minor

On pages 23 through to 25, number the scale degrees and add slurs to show where the half steps are and mark them with a 'h'.

How many half steps are there in a natural minor scale?

How many half steps are there in a harmonic minor scale?

On which scale degree in a harmonic scale would you find the two notes which are a whole step and a half?

Minor Arpeggios

Remember from Level 2, <u>arpeggios</u> are notes of a chord played one after another. We use the 1st, 3rd and 5th notes of a scale. We also include the 8th note.

Eg.

A minor   (A) B (C) D (E) F G (A)
            1   2   3   4   5   6 7   8

Circle the notes of the arpeggio of these scales below.

B minor

        B C# D E F# G A B

E minor

        E F# G A B C D E

Draw the arpeggio from these scales (using quarter notes) **in an <u>ascending</u> and <u>descending</u> order.**

B minor

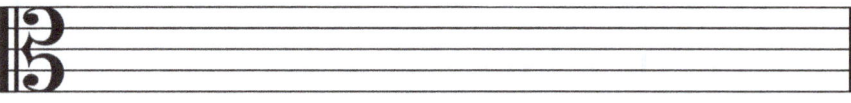

A minor

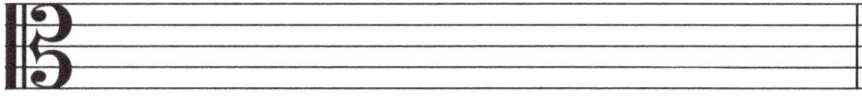

E minor

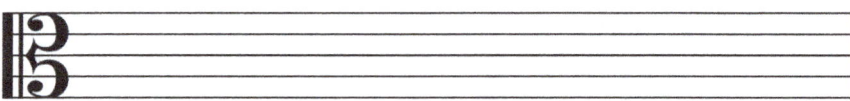

In whole notes, draw the same arpeggio scales in a descending and ascending order.

A minor

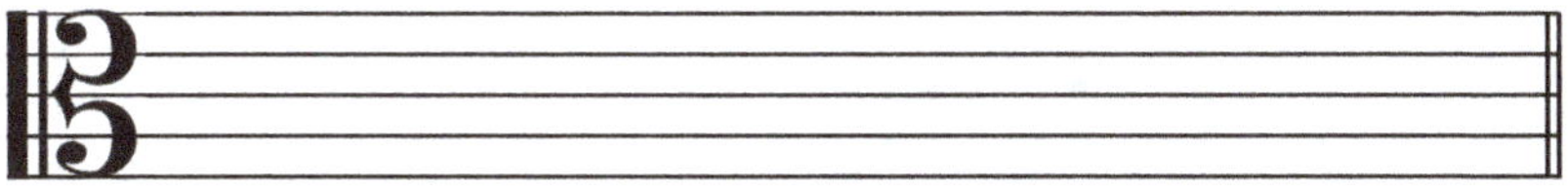

B minor

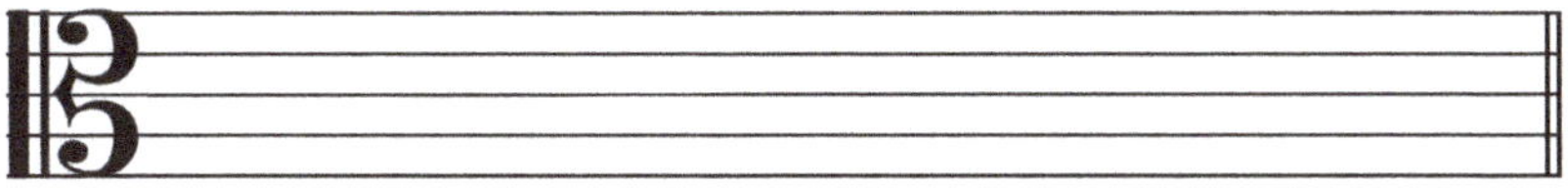

E minor

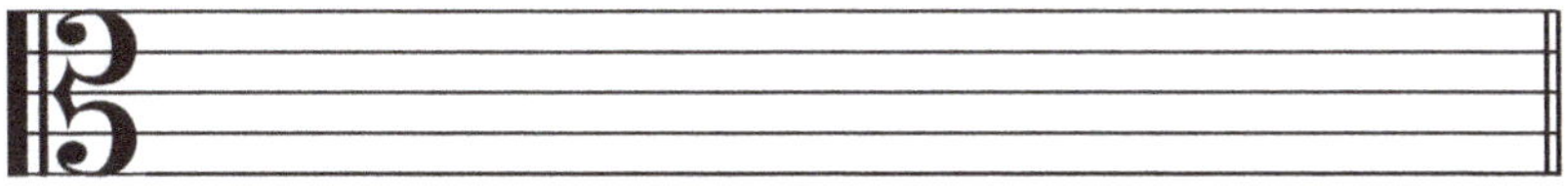

Now draw these scales (using half notes) **in an ascending and descending order.**

A melodic minor

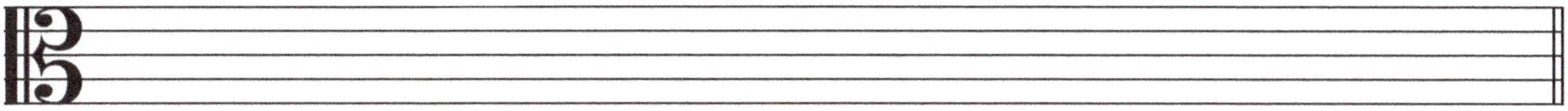

B melodic minor

E melodic minor

**Now try playing these scales on your viola.
Can you play these scales by memory? Let us try...**

Labeling Scales and Arpeggios

Label the scales and arpeggios below, then their movement.
(NOTE: Scales and arpeggios below are written with and without key signatures.)

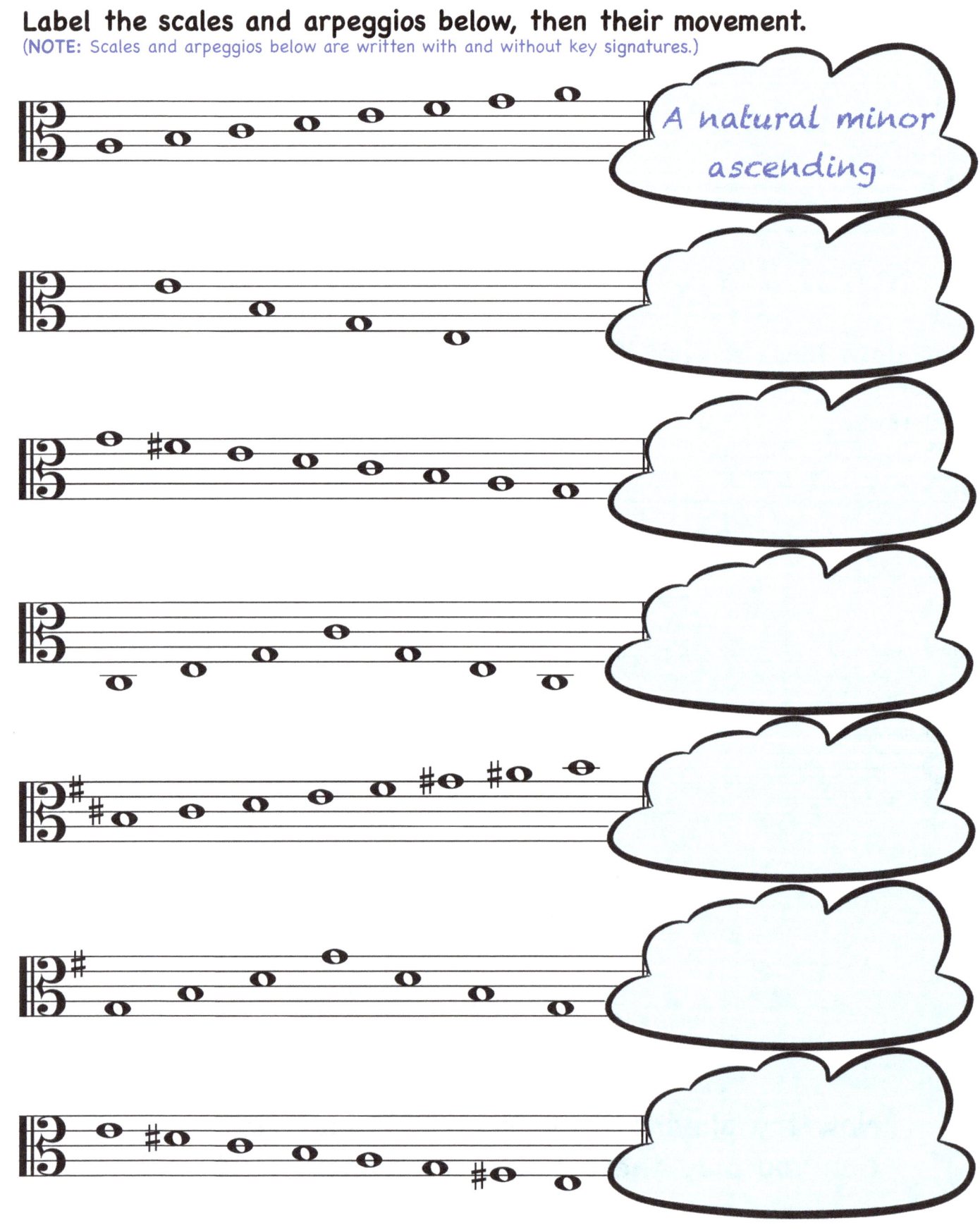

What have we learned so far?

Fill in the missing spaces on note values.

Note Name	Note	Note Value
si_t_en_h	♪	1/4
_i_tee_th re_t		
qua_t_r n_te		
e_gh_h no_te		
do___ed q_art_r not_		

Tommy just had his birthday party and has too many birthday cupcakes left over.
How many cupcakes did Tommy's friends take home?

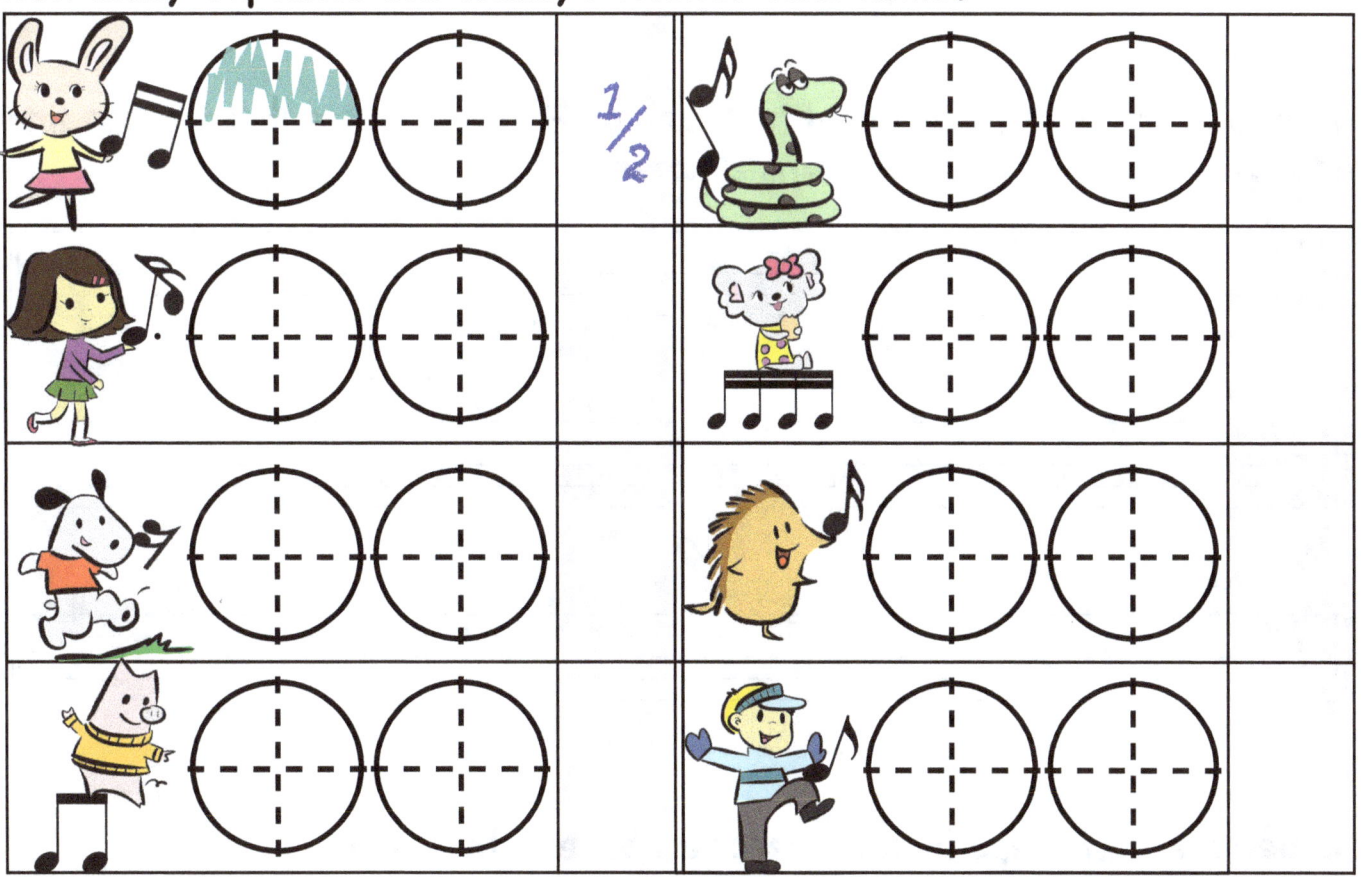

Clap and say the rhythms out loud.
Work out how many beats there are in each measure and write out the correct time signature.

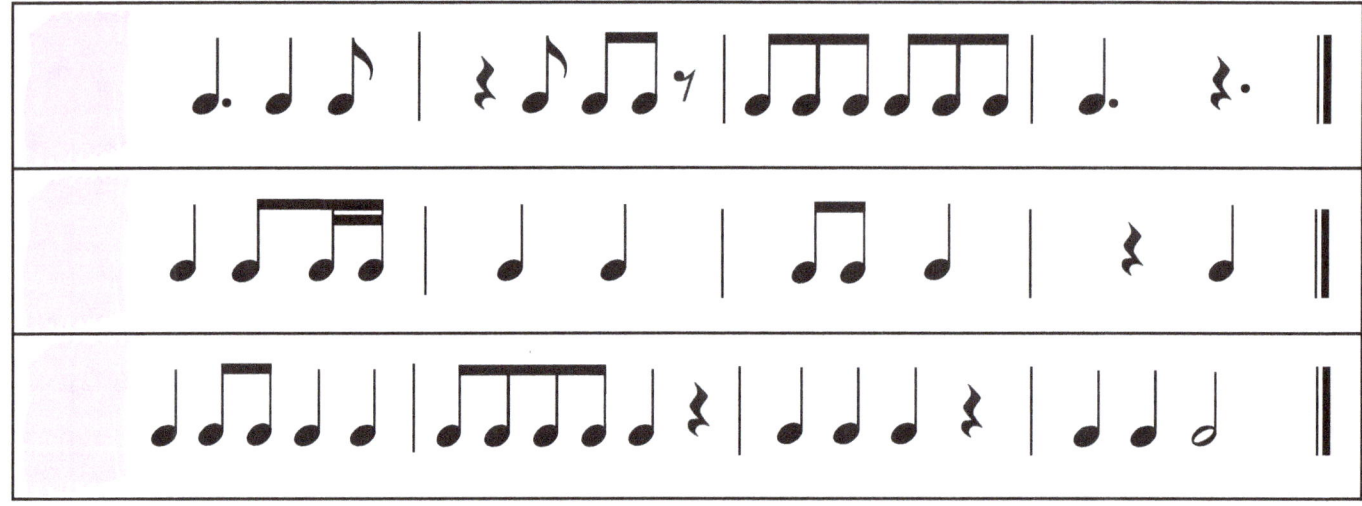

How many types of minor scales are there?

Name all the different quality types of minor scales available.

_____

_____

_____

Draw out the 3 different quality types of E minor scales in an ascending and descending order using whole notes.

Label the half steps in the exercise above with a slur.

Ostinato

An <u>ostinato</u> is a repeated rhythmic and pitch pattern.

Eg.

Draw 3 more ostinato patterns.

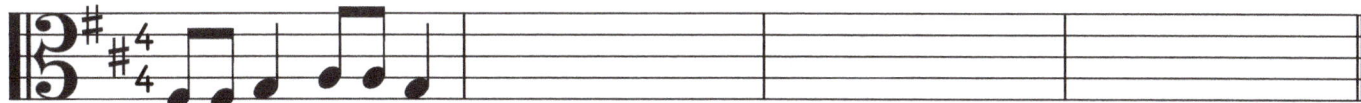

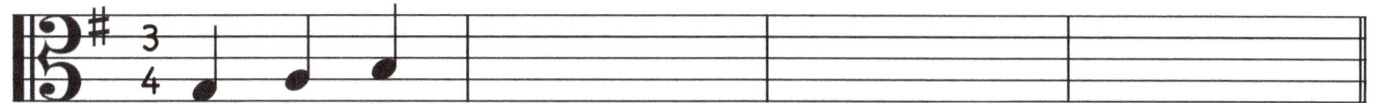

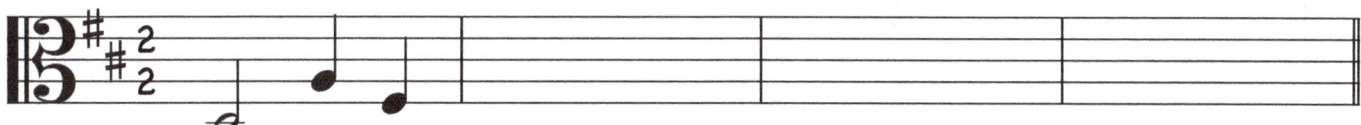

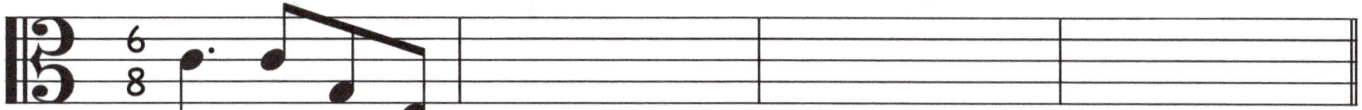

Ostinato vs. Sequence
Ostinato is a repeated rhythmic pattern with the same notes. Sequence is a repeated rhythmic and pitch pattern. It maintains the tune but moves the whole tune up or down.

Now try playing these ostinato pattern on your viola. Can you hear the difference between ostinato and sequence?

Sequences

A <u>sequence</u> is a melodic pattern that is repeated starting on a different note each time, either moving the whole pattern upwards or downwards.

Eg.

Draw a bracket (⌐¬) over each step of the sequence.

1.

2.

Make a sequence by repeating it twice, one note <u>higher</u> each time using the tune given.

Make a sequence by repeating it twice, one note <u>lower</u> each time using the tune given.

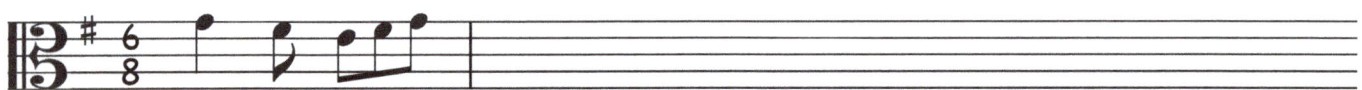

Now try playing these sequences on your viola. Can you hear how the tune moves?

Italian Terms

Expression Marking
Expression Marking tells a player in what kind of mood to play the music. They are written below the music.

    dolce - sweetly
    cantabile - in a singing style
    espressivo - expressively
    grazioso - gracefully
    leggiero - lightly
    molto - very

> Sometimes the way we remember meanings of terms is by looking at the first few letters of the music term. It is usually close to the english definition.

Tempo Marking
Tempo Marking tells a player in which speed to play the music.

Let us revise what we have learnt in Level 1 and 2 on Tempo. Fill in the blanks where needed.

    Vivace - fast and lively

    Allegro -

    Allegretto - quite fast (but slower then Allegro)

    Moderato -

    Andante -

    Adagio -

    Lento - slowly
    piu mosso - slower (less speed)
    meno mosso - faster (more speed)

34

Figure out the italian terms for the meanings below.

1. Moderate speed.
2. When you hold a note longer than its value.
3. Slowing down.
4. Fast.
5. Finish or the end.
6. Slow speed.
7. Same.
8. Short and detached.
9. Soft.
10. Sweetly.
11. Repeated pitch and rhythmic pattern.
12. Majestically.
13. Smoothly.
14. Getting softer.
15. Animated.
16. In a singing style.
17. Go back to the beginning.

Composition

There are many ways of composing music.

In Level 3, we learn how to write short tunes by using the first **FIVE** notes of a given scale to a given rhythm.

HINT: Start and end the tune using the FIRST note of the scale.

Eg. B minor

The first 5 notes for B minor are **B C♯ D E F♯**.
Below is one way we can write a tune using these notes.

Write a tune using the first **FIVE** notes of a given scale and rhythm.
(**REMINDER:** Write in the key and time signature.)

C major

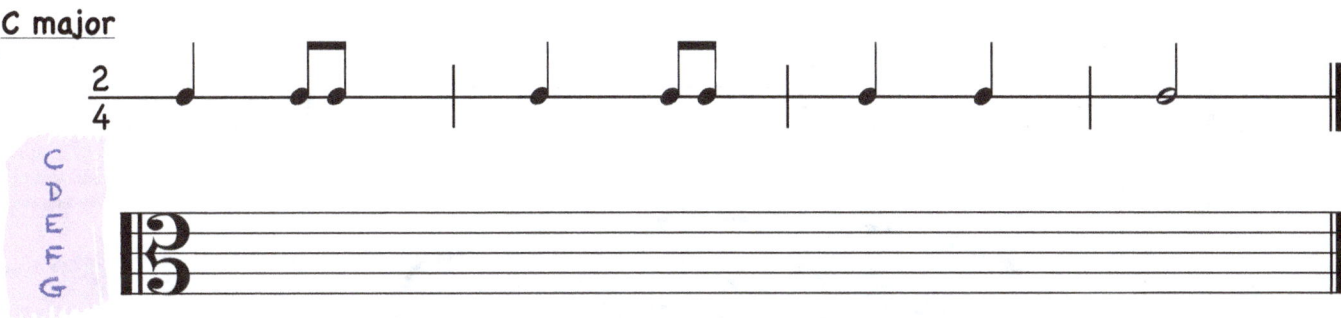

C D E F G

A minor

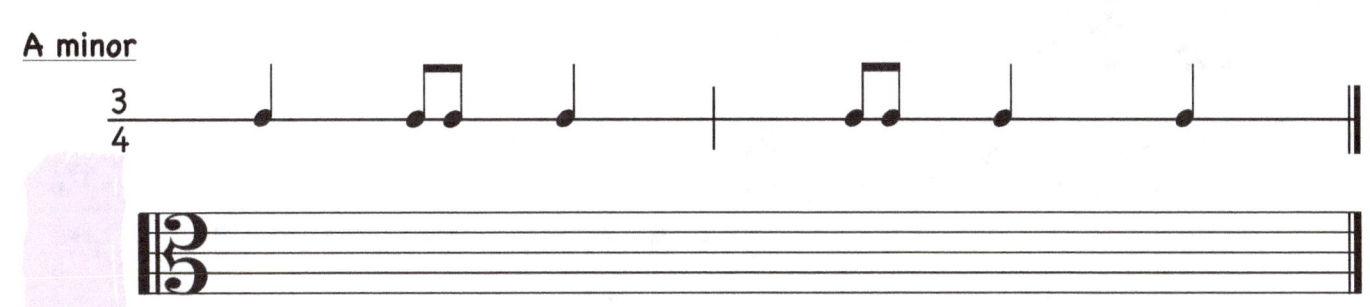

36

A minor

B minor

D major

G major

Did you remember to start each tune using the FIRST note of the scale?

**Now try playing these compositions which you have just written. Careful of the accidentals used.
Where do you lower your first and second finger in these short tunes?**

Anacrusis

An anacrusis is a note or a series of notes that comes before the first measure. It can also be referred to as an up-beat or pick-up.

As string players, we use an up-bow (∨) for a single up-beat note. This means that a down-bow (⊓) occurs on the first beat of the measure.

When you sing these tunes, notice how you emphasise more on the underlined words.

a- MAZ- ing   NOT A-maz-ing   NOT a-maz-ING

a- WAY   NOT A-way

Occasionally when you have more than one up-beat note, they do not always start with the up-bow.
Remember that the first beat of the first measure always starts with a down bow (⊓).

As shown below,

When a piece begins on an up-beat, the final measure has fewer beats than usual. The amount of beats in the anacrusis is taken out of the last measure to even out the difference.

The following rhythms begin with an anacrusis, but the note value on the last measure is <u>INCORRECT</u> (too many beats). **Rewrite the rhythm with the correct note value on the last measure.**

3rd Position

A knowledge of 3rd position will be useful for learning the information in this chapter.

Shifting
Shifting refers to the whole left hand moving smoothly up or down the fingerboard (like an escalator) to play notes in different positions on the fingerboard.

When we first started learning the viola, our hand position was close to the scroll. This is called the first position (the 1st finger on the first line of the fingering strip).

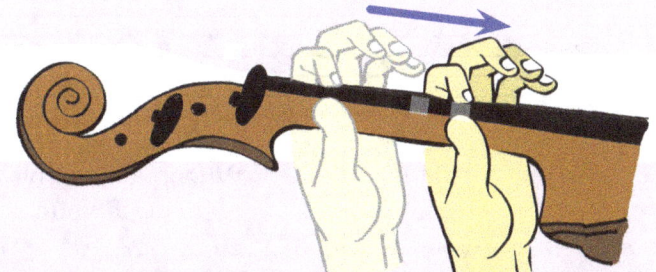

Different positions
A few new positions need to be learned. By now we should be 'experts' on the first position (original position).

In order to identify the other positions depends on where the first finger is placed. If the first finger is moved to the 2nd strip on the fingering board, you are now in 2nd position. If the 1st finger is moved to the 3rd line, you are now in 3rd position and so on.

Benefits:
- gain TWO new higher notes on each string
- more possibilities for fingerings to help play any tune
- help improve smooth playing of fast passages

Requirements:
- thumb is not left behind when fingers move
- control of finger spacing (whole step and half step)
- standing fingertip position enabling smaller spacing
- elbow moves

We use Roman Numerals to mark the different positions which is shown below,

        I - First Position
       II - Second Position
     III - Third Position
    IV - Fourth Position
     V - Fifth Position

Below is a short exercise to practice shifting between first position and third position on the A string. Practise it slowly.

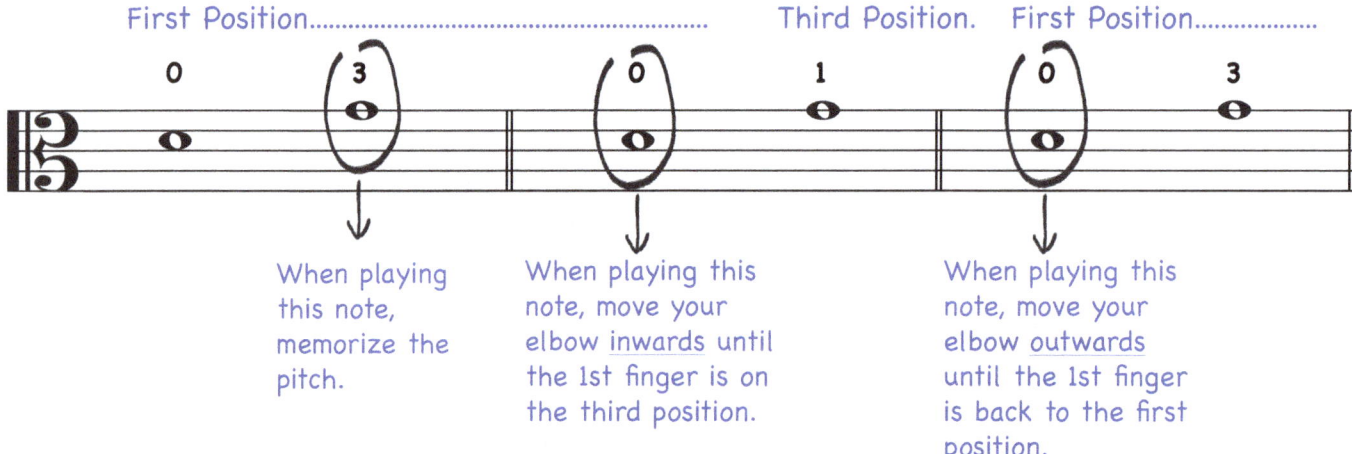

Now play this exercise on the other strings.

Remember when shifting,
1. Thumb follows movement of the whole arm
2. Elbow moves outwards and inwards
3. Loosen hold when shifting between positions

When playing a ONE octave scale on the third position, you can always use the whole step and half step pattern we learned on a typical major scale.

W - W - h - W - W - W - h

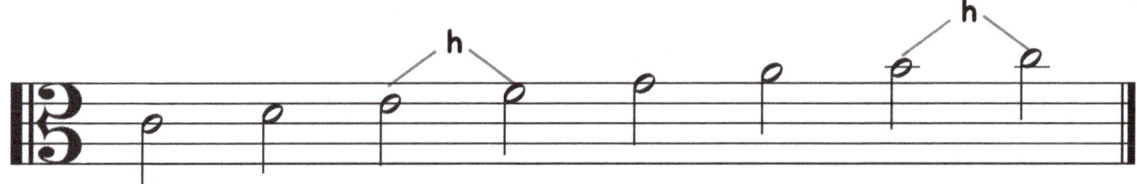

Simon Says.....

Let us play SLOWLY on the D string.

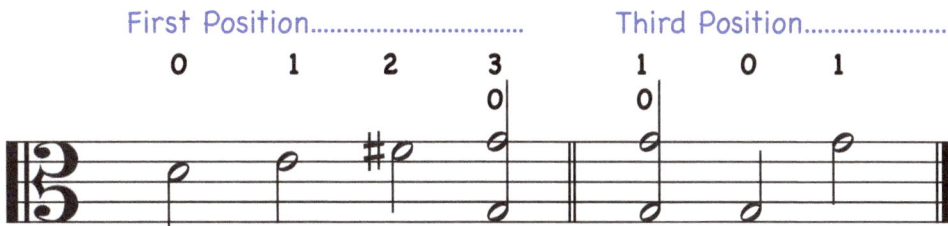

1. Place the 3rd finger down in the first position.
2. Play all the other notes on the D string until you reach the G note (3rd finger).
3. Play the note and compare it to the lower open string (G string).
4. Replace the 3rd finger with the 1st finger by loosening your finger hold and moving your whole wrist (including the thumb) up the fingerboard.

(**NOTE:** Wrist has to be straight.)

5. Place the first finger down.
6. Play the note and listen to the pitch. Compare the pitch with the lower open string.

YAY!! Congratulations. You have arrived in 3rd position.

7. Now play a scale in the 3rd position using your other fingers as shown below.
Always compare notes to the neighboring string.

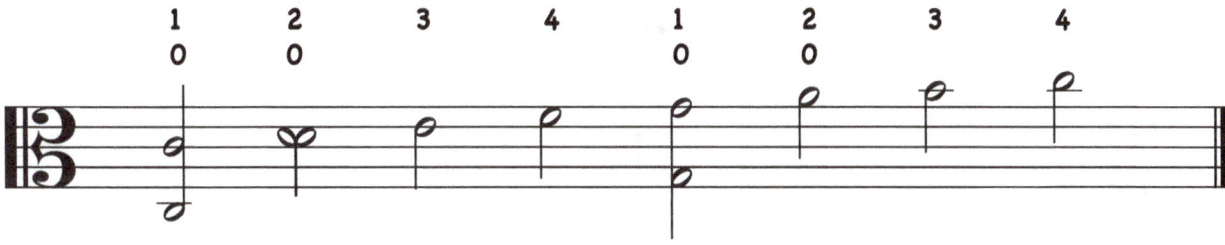

Were you successful?

(**REMINDER:** On any major scale, half steps are between the 3rd+4th and 7th+8th notes. This means that when you play these 2 notes consecutively, your fingers have to be right next to each other to produce the correct pitch.)

8. If yes, let us try playing the same exercise on the D string.

Last Revision

1. Cross out the answers which are incorrect.

leggiero	lightly	~~smoothly~~
Vivace	viper	fast and lively
grazioso	gorilla	gracefully
A minor	has ONE sharp	has no sharps or flats
ostinato	repeated pitch and rhythmic pattern	repeated rhythmic pattern

2. Write a tune using the first FIVE notes of a given scale and rhythm.
   (**REMINDER:** Write in the key signature and time signature.)

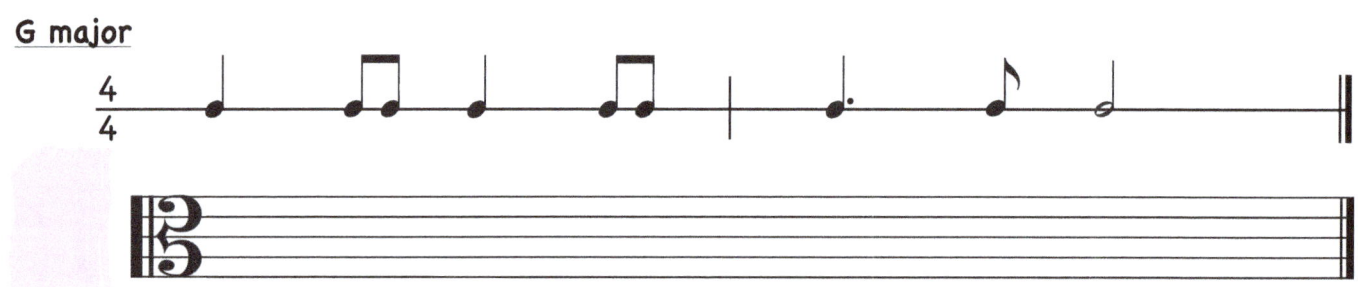

3. Draw the key signature of these minor keys.

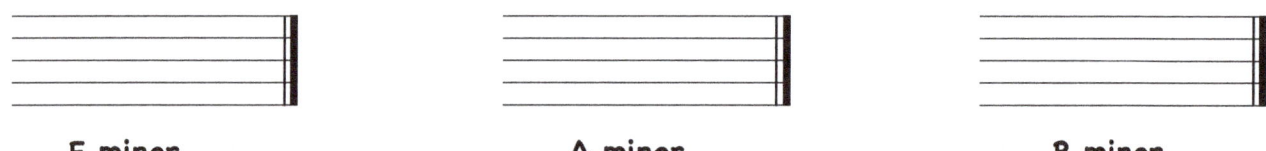

E minor   A minor   B minor

4. **Write out the D harmonic scale using the correct key signature.**
   - Draw the alto clef
   - One octave ascending only
   - Use whole notes
   - Complete the scale with a double bar line

5. Help Suzie decorate the Christmas tree using the different colored ornaments mentioned accordingly.

½ count	1 count	2 counts	3 counts
yellow	red	blue	orange

6. **What do these time signatures mean?**

   3/4 _3 quarter beats in a bar_

   2/2 _____

   6/8 _____

44

Name: _____ Date: _____

 www.stringstastic.com

Test

TOTAL MARKS: _____/100

1. **Name these notes.** (Use capital letters.) _____/9

2. In first position, write out the correct fingering above the notes in question 1. _____/9

3. Match the major and minor keys to its correct key signature. _____/6

C major      B minor

D major   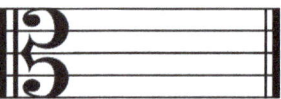   A minor

G major   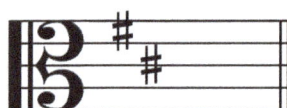   E minor

4. What are the definitions of these words. _____/8

    A. *grazioso*

    B. *dolce*

    C. *cantabile*

    D. *espressivo*

5. Write out these scales using the correct key signature. _____/20

E harmonic minor
- Draw the treble clef
- One octave descending only
- Use quarter notes
- Complete the scale with a double bar line

A melodic minor
- Draw the treble clef
- One octave in an ascending and descending order
- Use half notes
- Complete the scale with a double bar line

D major arpeggio
- Draw the treble clef
- One octave in an ascending and descending order
- Use whole notes
- Complete the scale with a double bar line

B minor arpeggio
- Draw the treble clef
- One octave in a descending and ascending order
- Use eighth notes in pairs
- Complete the scale with a double bar line

46

6. Using the key signature of G major, write a tune using the first FIVE notes of the scale. _____/6

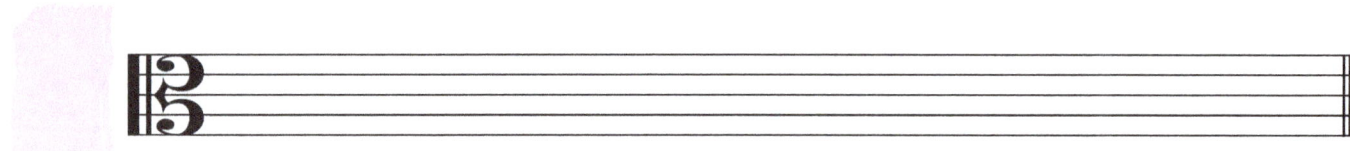

7. Tick the correct definition of these words below. _____/2

   A. An ostinato is a ......
      ○ repeated balancing act
      ○ repeated rhythmic pattern but moves up or down by one note each time
      ○ repeated rhythmic and pitch pattern

   B. Sequence is a ......
      ○ repeated balancing act
      ○ repeated rhythmic pattern but moves up or down by one note each time
      ○ repeated rhythmic and pitch pattern

8. Fill in the blanks. _____/30

	Dynamic or Tempo	Written above or below the music	Definition
Vivace			
crescendo			
Adagio			
meno mosso			
mezzo forte			

9. Answer the questions below.

A. How many

B. How many pairs of

C. How many

D. How many

___/4

10. How many counts should the last note be in the rhythm given below?   ___/2

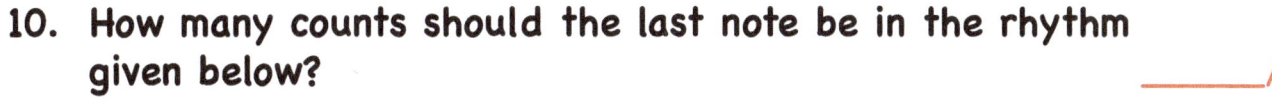

11. Circle the anacrusis on the rhythm in question 10.   ___/2

12. Write in the bow marking on the first note on question 10.   ___/2

www.ingramcontent.com/pod-product-compliance
Lightning Source LLC
Chambersburg PA
CBHW080856010526
44107CB00057B/2599